TD's Drum Book

Creative Solo Music for the Drum Set

By Tim Daisy

Relay Documents 001

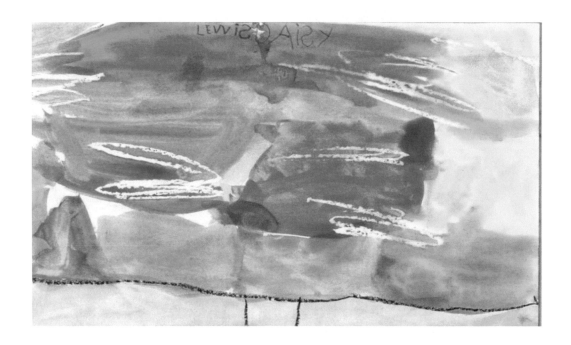

Creative Solo Music for the Drum Set
By Tim Daisy

First Edition

ISBN (Print Edition): 979-8-35094-004-6
ISBN (eBook Edition): 979-8-35094-005-3

Relay Documents 001
Relay Recordings, Chicago, IL www.timdaisyrelayrecordings.bandcamp.com
Artwork by Lewis Daisy
Photos by Tim Daisy

CONTENTS

ACKNOWLEDGEMENTS

I want to express my deep and sincere gratitude to those who helped me put the ideas in this book into a concrete and discernable format. A special thanks goes to the artist, improviser, and educator Lou Mallozzi for his creative guidance, helpful editing suggestions, and his generosity with his time. I am much obliged. A big round of applause also goes to Joseph Clayton Mills for suggesting a few structural and aesthetic issues and for his proofreading expertise. To Olivia Junell, Adam Vida, Alex Inglizian, and Ralph Loza at the Experimental Sound Studio in Chicago for giving me a home to record so much music on the drums over the past two decades. The same debt of gratitude goes to Nick Broste, Todd Carter, and Bill Harris for traveling to my home numerous times to help document some of my solo and collaborative work in sound. To my life partner, Emma Daisy, I could not do any of this without you, and to my kids, Lewis and Nina, you light up my life in so many ways. And finally, to my parents, Mary and Don Daisy, who bought me my first drum set at the tender age of thirteen. My life has never been the same since.

PREFACE

The ideas presented in this book are designed for anyone looking to engage in creating solo music on the drum set, whether approaching the art form for the first time or looking to gain fresh perspectives on an already-established practice. My intent in presenting these concepts is to inspire the reader to develop a wide range of tools one can call upon during a performance situation, encouraging new avenues of sound exploration by offering diverse ideas and approaches.

These exercises are intended to be applied within the context of improvisation and are geared toward folks with at least some experience with the concept. However, even if you are entirely new to the art form, I hope these concepts encourage new perspectives on whatever sound-making format you are currently involved with. Perhaps these ideas can also be a catalyst that sparks interest in forging a relationship with improvisation.

It is important to add that, although the solo format is the vehicle in which the ideas in this work were built, I do not intend any of them to be exclusive to this configuration. If you can find ways to apply any of the information herein in a collaborative context of any size, or if any of these ideas inspire a through-composed work on the drum set (or even another instrument), I would be delighted.

This book is organized into three main parts:

THE 20-BPM METRONOME EXERCISE

I have developed the 20-bpm metronome exercise and a few variations on it as a warm-up to engage in slow practice while using all four limbs on the kit. I have found it to be quite helpful for various reasons, one of them being that it is a great way to get your mind and body in sync and to help remove some of the "background noise" currently surrounding our media-saturated lives. Another benefit I have found is that, by practicing slowly, one gains insight into techniques that might need improvement, and aspects of one's performance that might otherwise go unnoticed become apparent. My intention is for this metronome exercise to encourage the artist to get into a concentrated head space before moving on to the ideas in the next chapter.

CREATIVE IDEAS FOR SOLO MUSIC ON THE DRUM SET

In this chapter, I have presented twenty studies, concepts, ideas, thoughts, and instructions for you to memorize, reflect upon, and utilize in the context of solo improvisation. Some of these concepts are clear and straightforward, while others are purposefully vague, as I encourage multiple interpretations and perspectives. Only one of the ideas in this chapter includes traditional music notation, and it is used only as a suggestive example. You do not need to be able to read music to gain benefit from any of the ideas presented here or elsewhere throughout this book.

RESOURCES AND INSPIRATION

In Resources and Inspiration, I offer a listening guide to some of my favorite recordings of solo drum set music. This is a partial list, as I am sure I have left out many excellent recordings that deserve inclusion. The ones included here are ones that I connect with on a deep listening level and find myself returning to for inspiration regularly. You'll also find a section titled 'Living Heroes' which lists some of my favorite drummers whom I have had the great pleasure not only to listen to but to engage with, share stories, and at times perform with at one point or another during my twenty-plus years working in the field of improvised music. These are the folks whose contributions to the art of drumming inspire me to keep moving forward with my work. A huge debt of gratitude is owed to every one of them; I cannot thank them enough.

Lastly, I have included a page on recommended reading: articles, books, and interviews connected to the history of the drum set, the art of improvisation, and various performers and creative thinkers who continue to experiment and push improvised music in a forward direction.

I have included a contact email on the bio page. Please don't hesitate to contact me if you have any questions about the exercises or suggestions for clarity or improvement. I would love to hear from you.

Many thanks for your time and curiosity!

Tim Daisy
Evanston, IL

'Solo Drum' by Lewis Daisy Age 6

Solo setup/Narwhal Studios Chicago, IL

THE 20-BPM METRONOME EXERCISE

INTRODUCTION

This metronome exercise was first shown to me many years ago as a warm-up to be played on the snare drum. I have found it primarily effective in two ways: in helping to develop a deeper awareness of time by meditating on a slow pulse, and in conditioning the hands by working through various subdivisions of the underlying beat. It was originally shown to me with the metronome pulse set at 40 bpm.

Confident in its effectiveness at strengthening time awareness, concentration, and conditioning, I have decided to expand upon the exercise and have developed some ways to apply it to all four limbs on the drum set. I have also slowed the recommended metronome pulse down from 40 bpm to 20 bpm for an added physical and mental challenge.

Try to be patient and work through this warm-up at an unhurried pace. Focused engagement is the goal. Doing this warm-up for 10 minutes while paying complete attention is much more effective than doing it for an hour or more while checking social media or engaging in other forms of "multitasking."

In this chapter, I have outlined a few ways you can execute this exercise using both the hands and the feet on the drum set. The concept is clear, but as you will see, it takes a bit of mental dexterity to pull off. Try to stay relaxed and aim to maintain an even sound on all four limbs. Don't get discouraged; I have yet to make it through one iteration of this exercise without anticipating a downbeat or landing ahead or behind when moving through the subdivisions.

I encourage everyone to begin with Exercise A, Four-Limb Unison, before moving on to the additional applications I have outlined.

The four-limb variations that I have developed are by no means the only available options. You should get creative and devise additional ways to apply this concept on the drums, or on any musical instrument, for that matter. I will also mention that, although the exercise was developed and intended for all four limbs, this warm-up is completely adaptable as needed for any differently abled person who chooses to engage with it.

On page 10, I have offered a notated version of the warm-up, with the metronome pulse indicated with an x above each subdivision. Feel free to use this as a guide if you find it helpful.

THE 20-BPM METRONOME EXERCISE

PART 1

Set the metronome to 20 bpm.

Begin this exercise by playing with both hands and feet together in unison, starting with one beat for each metronome pulse. Go for an even dynamic between all four limbs.

rf = bass drum / lf = high-hat / rh = floor tom or ride cymbal / lh = snare drum

After locking into the metronome pulse at 20 bpm, divide the beat into 2, 3, 4, 5, 6, 7, and 8 beat divisions per pulse. Move forward only when the number of beats you are subdividing is locked in and feels good.

Once you have reached 8 unison strokes for one metronome pulse, work in reverse, moving from 8 back down to 1, again moving back only when the timing is locked in.

Below is a number guide that you can focus on while working through the exercise.

1 2 3 4 5 6 7 8 7 6 5 4 3 2 1

This first part of the metronome exercise can be considered a meditation on the drum set. Stay relaxed and focus on one sound with all four limbs while moving through the subdivisions.

THE 20-BPM METRONOME EXERCISE

PART 2

Set the metronome to 20 bpm.

The same method described in part 1 applies here. All four limbs play in unison through various subdivisions of the slow metronome pulse. The one difference here is that you should skip through various subdivisions randomly instead of working through them chronologically.

Here are some examples of possible roadmaps:

1 4 7 2 1 6 3 8

4 3 6 5 3 1 4 2

5 1 6 2 7 3 4 1

3 2 1 4 5 6 7 8

I encourage you to develop as many sequences as you can. Feel free to make these sequences longer or shorter. More examples are given below.

2 1 8

8 4 6 4

1 8 2 7 3 6 4 5 8 1 7 2 6 3 5 4 1

1 5 2 5 3 5 4 5 8

5 6

8 7 1 2 6 5 3 4 3 5 6 2 1 7

2 3 2 4 2 5 2 6

1 2 1 3 8 7 8 6 5 4 1

There are an infinite number of possibilities created by moving around the sequence randomly. Mapping them out can be helpful, but I also encourage you to move randomly in an improvised way. Choose your own adventure, so to speak.

THE 20-BPM METRONOME EXERCISE

ADDITIONAL APPLICATIONS

I have outlined a few more possibilities you can explore using the 20-bpm metronome exercise. These are only some of the available approaches, and I encourage you to find new and creative ways to work through the concept.

1.

Feet play one beat (alternating rf/lf or lf/rf) for each metronome pulse. Both hands move through the exercise (1–8 and 8–1) in unison.

2.

Feet play two beats (alternating) for each metronome pulse. Hands move through the exercise (1–8 and 8–1) in unison.

The feet can continue by subdividing 3 through 8 divisions while alternating. (By the way, you'll notice that things start to get interesting when the feet are alternating in group 5 while the unison hands are climbing between 3, 4, 5, 6, and 7).

3.

Hands alternate (rh/lh or lh/rh) one beat per metronome pulse. Both feet move (1–8 and 8–1) in unison.

Hands alternate (rh/lh or lh/rh) two beats per metronome pulse. Both feet move (1–8 and 8–1) in unison.

The hands can continue the process of subdividing subdivisions 3 through 8 while alternating.

4.

Hands and feet move in a linear fashion.

Play one beat using one limb at a time for each metronome pulse. Move in a clockwise fashion (rh/rf/lf/lh). Play one beat using one limb at a time in a counterclockwise fashion (rh/lh/lf/rf).

Play one beat using one limb at a time randomly.

5.

Increase subdivision of beats.

Use the sequence below to further subdivide the beat into groupings of 9, 10, 11, and 12.

1 2 3 4 5 6 7 8 9 10 11 12

THE 20-BPM METRONOME EXERCISE

x = metronome pulse

CREATIVE IDEAS FOR SOLO MUSIC ON THE DRUM SET

INTRODUCTION

This chapter includes a set of twenty ideas that can be utilized, reflected upon, and applied within the context of solo performance on the drum set. Many of these concepts may also be helpful in various collaborative contexts, and I encourage you to work with them as you see fit. The focus here is on solo performance.

I do not claim ownership over any ideas presented in this chapter. None of them fell out of the sky. Even if my take or perspective on a concept seems unique to me, I am pretty sure it has been adapted from something I was shown at a lesson or rehearsal, saw at a concert, or picked up by listening to, conversing, and exchanging ideas with many of the great improvising musicians that I have been lucky enough to meet. The only authorship I can claim connected to any of this work is my honest attempt to present these ideas through the lens of solo drum set performance.

My philosophy connected to improvising continues to evolve. However, one element that has remained consistent is keeping a clear and open mind, starting with a blank canvas, and not mapping out events in advance. I like letting my ideas unfold organically and allowing sounds and silences to occur naturally. I'm only sometimes successful at this, and the idea of what success means is subjective. But my goal has been and continues to be to present a solo work on the drum set where the ideas feel unforced, flow easily from one to the next, and cover a variety of sonic landscapes. Keeping a clear head at the outset of each performance has been the best way for me to achieve the desired outcomes. It is important to note that it has taken me years to develop my solo vocabulary, and I am always inviting new elements into my language. Permission to be free in a solo concert has been granted to me through many hours of practice and experimentation.

I also add that many great improvisers work within various compositional frameworks: composed fragments, lead sheets, graphic scores, and conduction. All of it is valid, and it is highly inspiring. I have been lucky to have gotten to work in a variety of these contexts myself, and I am genuinely grateful for the opportunities.

I developed almost all these ideas using a four-piece kit, usually with an 18" or 20" bass drum, 12" rack tom, 14" floor tom (with legs), and 14" snare drum (all fitted with coated heads). I usually employ a set of high-hats, two ride cymbals, and, at times, a third small cymbal of various shapes and sizes on my right side, just under the ride cymbal. You can use whatever drum setup you see fit, but I wanted to give you a bit of context as to what I used when I developed these ideas.

1. TEXTURES AND REPEATED FIGURES

Coated drumheads are recommended for this exercise. Using brushes or hands, maintain a static textural sound on the snare with the left hand and on the floor tom with the right hand; use a circular motion to create the textures.

Invent an ostinato or repeated figure for your feet to play, with your left foot on the high hat and right foot on the bass drum. Repeat this foot pattern under the static textural sounds. The foot pattern can be in a metered time or a repeated out-of-time gesture. Experiment with a variety of tempos and patterns.

Additional options:

Increase or decrease the textural density by manipulating the brush or hands to increase or decrease the among of surface area contact with the drumhead.

Create small circles that evolve into larger circles, and vice versa, while the foot ostinato remains unchanged.

Shift randomly between playing only with your hands and playing only with your feet. Foot ostinato can gradually speed up or slow down.

Foot ostinato can get louder and then softer. Make brief pauses in playing with the hands and/or the feet.

2. CHANGING CHANNELS

The "changing channels" concept involves shifting from one sound-making area to another with intention and clarity, in a manner similar to channels changing on television. The idea here is to jump into a new territory of sound cleanly and without hesitation.

This concept is especially effective when focusing on contrasts between channels—for example, when a loud and dense landscape shifts into a quiet texture. Busy, low-volume, ride cymbal gestures change into a loud march-like feel on the snare drum. There are a lot of options you can explore.

One application of this concept that I have found helpful is listed below.

Develop three or four contained sonic landscapes you can memorize and use as content for your "channel." Shift between these various channels randomly, varying the durations each time you make a change.

Below is a list of possible ideas for your landscapes to use as content. I use phrases such as "two-hand unison figure" and "morse code with hands," knowing they are slightly open-ended or vague. I do this purposefully, as I trust you to use your imagination and invent your way of interpreting them on the drum set.

1. Static texture on any drum or cymbal
2. Single repetition on any drum or cymbal
3. Repeated melodic phrases on the toms
4. Two-hand unison figure on the floor tom and snare
5. Two-feet unison figure on the bass drum and high-hat
6. Four-limb unison figure
7. One hand or one foot (isolated)
8. Loud, isolated hits on any drum
9. Soft, isolated hits on any drum
10. Improvise on the rims of the snare or floor tom
11. Steady pulse on any drum or cymbal

Additional options:

Experiment with the rapidity of the channel changes, alternating quick changes with slow changes and vice versa.

Explore dynamics within a given channel and when changing the channel.

Move through your various channels in a predetermined sequence: 1, 2, 3, 4, 3, 2, 1 or 1, 3, 2, 4, 3, 1, 4, 2, for example.

Change the channel only once during the improvisation.

3. LIMITATION AS A MECHANISM FOR INVENTION

Focus your attention on one select area of the drum set, such as the floor tom and ride cymbal, the high-hat and rack tom, or the snare drum, crash cymbal, and bass drum. Improvise for any length of time on the selected area of focus. Move to a new area of focus and improvise for any length of time. Continue this concept for as long as you can. Explore various available combinations of instruments and develop new ideas by limiting yourself to these selected areas of the kit.

What discoveries have you made? What are some new approaches you have developed?

"Our thoughts and imaginations are the only real limits to our possibilities."
-Orison Swett Marden

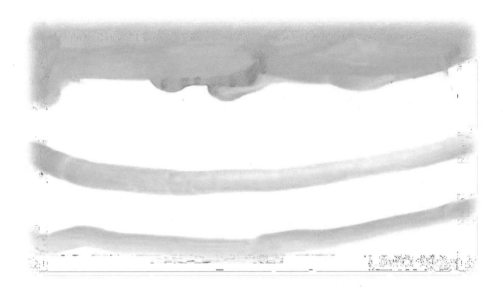

4. FOCUS ON DURATION

Using a timer or stopwatch, improvise for a predetermined length of time. Vary the durations of each improvisation. You could begin with 2 minutes; switch to 30 seconds. The next improvisation could be 3 minutes and 12 seconds. Twelve minutes? Thirty? Twelve seconds?

It's totally up to you.

The idea here is to investigate time awareness by exploring a range of fixed durations. This is excellent practice to help analyze pacing and create new ideas, as the limited available time often helps create new ideas out of necessity.

Additional options:

Each improvised duration focuses on one drum or cymbal.

Each improvised duration focuses on the development of one idea. Change dynamics for each improvised duration.

One duration is a study developing a single idea. One duration is a study developing multiple ideas.

Challenge yourself by beginning each improvisation with an idea that contrasts with the end of the previous one.

NOTES:

5. STICK SELECTION AS FORM

Sticks, brushes, and mallets create a form.

Arrange sticks, brushes, and mallets in a predetermined order. Use this sequence as the form for the improvisation. The improvising is entirely up to you. The only guide is the order in which you decide to use the tools.

A few examples:

Begin with mallets, then move to brushes, over to sticks, and back to mallets.

Begin with hands, then move to sticks, over to mallets, back to hands, and end with brushes.

Begin with one mallet and one hand, then move to both hands, then to one brush and one hand, and end with both hands.

Begin with sticks, move over to brushes, then to mallets, and end with one mallet and one brush.

Begin with one brush and one stick, then one mallet and one stick, then one mallet and one brush, and end with both hands.

Begin with sticks, move to hands, over to brushes, over to sticks, and end with mallets.

Additional options:

Combine the "stick selection as form" idea with the "changing channels concept" to inspire a solo work.

Explore other sound-making devices that you could add to the mix: knitting needles, chopsticks, rattles, forks, and chains. (Knives, however, are not recommended!)

Maintain one core idea while switching through the various selections of sticks, mallets, and brushes.

Explore various levels of dynamics within each area of the form.

What are some more ways that you can utilize this concept to create some new ideas?

6. THREE METRONOMES

1. Shifting between multiple tempos and exploring the idea of sound collage.
2. Set up three metronome pulses. Suggested tempos: slow (*andante* 80 bpm), medium (*moderato* 110 bpm), and fast (*allegro* 140 bpm).

Turn on all three metronomes, activating the three pulses.

Warm-up:

Focus your attention on the slow pulse (80 bpm) and improvise along with it in time. Focus your attention on the medium pulse (110 bpm) and improvise along with it in time. Focus your attention on the fast pulse (140 bpm) and improvise along with it in time.

Make sure all three metronomes continue while you move between the three separate tempos. Avoid letting the other metronomes distract you from the tempo on which you are focusing.

What you choose to play while focusing on the separate tempos in this exercise is entirely up to you. However, pay close attention to whichever tempo you are working with, stay locked into it, and try not to get knocked around or distracted by the sounds of the other tempos.

The next steps:

A. Continue with all three metronomes turned on. Begin to improvise by jumping randomly between the slow, medium, and fast pulses. Vary the length of time you spend in each tempo.
B. Experiment with playing free time parallel to the three metronome pulses but not locking into any tempos. This can create a push/pull tension and a collage of sounds that can be interesting to navigate and explore.
C. Move between A and B above. Play for a set period in one or more of the tempos, and at times, shift away and play free in parallel with the metronomes.

Additional options:

Create a sequence for how you will work through the tempos (e.g., slow/fast/free/medium; slow/ free/slow/fast/medium/free; fast/slow/fast/medium/slow).

Hands follow one tempo, feet follow another.

One hand is on slow tempo, one is on medium tempo, and both feet are on fast tempo (or any variations on this idea). Explore various tempos with the metronomes.

Increase the number of metronomes to 4, 5, 6, or more.

7. REVERSE SET UP

If you are right-handed, set the drums up left-handed: the high-hat and snare drum on your right side, the bass drum and floor tom on your left side. (If using a four-piece kit, the rack tom would be just above the snare drum and perhaps a bit to the left.)

If you are left-handed, set the drums up right-handed: the high-hat and snare drum on your left side, the bass drum and floor tom on your right side. (The rack tom would be above the snare and a bit to the right if using a four-piece kit.)

Reverse the ride and crash cymbals in each case.

It will probably feel a bit awkward to play the drums set up "backward" at first. And that's the point. This exercise should pull you out of your comfort zone and force you to rethink a whole range of ideas that you've developed as a right-handed or left-handed player.

After practicing this way, set the drums back to your normal playing position. You may be surprised at how the weaker side of your body has been exercised and strengthened, and as a result, all four limbs may feel more in balance.

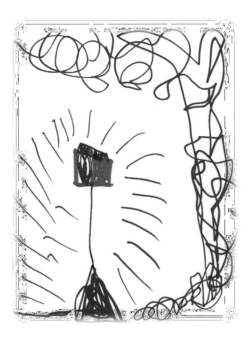

8. BUILDING BLOCKS

Determine three or more recognizable areas of sound-making that you can utilize during an improvisation. Use these as your core ideas or building blocks, memorize them, and move in and out of them in any order. The form can be predetermined or created during the improvisation.

Feel free to develop the ideas within each area of sound you choose for your building blocks; however, when returning to a previous building block, replicate the initial idea you started with.

Each building block should have a recognizable sonic identity that can be easily identified when you return to it.

A few potential tools to create areas of sound with:

Repetition
Texture
Melody
Fragments
Morse code
High density/low volume
Low density/high volume
Focus on one instrument
Hands only
Feet only
Long sounds (cymbal drones/buzz rolls)
Short sounds (single hits on the snare drum or rim of the floor tom)
Isolated attacks on any drum or cymbal
Contrasts: High-pitch sounds/low-pitch sounds
        High volume/low volume
        High density/low density
        Slow patterns/fast patterns

Additional options:

Combine this exercise with the "focus on duration" in chapter 4. Set up a predetermined length of time in which to move through the four areas of sound.

Assign each building block a number, then write out a predetermined form to use during the improvisation.

Use silence as one of your blocks.

NOTES:

9. REORCHESTRATE RHYTHMIC PATTERNS

Main idea: The rhythmic pattern is fixed, but the sound sources are not.

Repeat rhythmic patterns using any combination of drums or cymbals (open repeat). Reorchestrate which drums and cymbals you play when changing measures.

5

These nine measures can be used as your foundational rhythmic patterns. Feel free to repeat each measure as many times as you like until moving on. Explore various tempos.

In addition, this exercise can be practiced without using the above template. Feel free to develop your own rhythmic cells to work with. The idea is to explore various timbres on the drums while utilizing a fixed rhythmic pattern.

10. MORSE CODE

Use short and long sounds to create "Morse code" style patterns around the drums. Experiment with dynamics and tempo. Keep the short and long sounds consistent to achieve clarity.

Some examples of possible short and long sound ideas and an illustration of short and long patterns inspired by Morse code are below.

1. Short sounds

    - Finger taps on the snare drum
    - Metal rims of the snare drum, rack tom, or floor tom played with sticks or back of wire brushes
    - Hold the ride or crash cymbal with one hand to prevent ringing; strike the cymbal with a drumstick or brush
    - High-hat cymbals in closed position
    - "Dead sticking." Press the tip of the drumstick(s) into the drumhead to create a short, nonresonant sound
    - Use a closed fist to knock on top of the bass drum

2. Long sounds

    - Static texture on the snare drum (coated head) using brushes or hands
    - Cymbal rolls with mallets
    - Buzz roll with sticks on the snare drum
    - Open tuning on the bass drum
    - Open tuning on the floor tom and rack tom
    - Cymbal overtone with a stick

_____ • _____ •• _____ ••• _____ • •• ••

_____ • _____ ••• • ••• • _____ _____ ••

• _____

11. BODY AND VOICE

Making connections between what you sing and what you play.

Sing a melody from a popular tune, a jazz standard, or a nursery rhyme, or even make something up. The aim is to examine how vocal phrasing connects to drum set phrasing and how this concept can offer a fresh approach to improvisation.

Here are three methods to use to explore the connections between body and voice:

1. Direct connection: Play the rhythmic shape of the melody you sing around the drums in the most literal way possible. Feel free to reorchestrate which drums and/or cymbals you play; however, stick as close as possible to the melody.

2. Abstract connection: Imply the rhythmic shape of the melody on the drums, but feel free to deviate from it. Add outside elements into the mix. Create counter rhythms, add textures, and use silence. Make sure you continue to sing the melody out loud while pushing and pulling away from it on the kit.

3. Contrast: While singing the melody out loud, improvise around the drums in a way that is not at all connected to the song's melodic content. The improvising is created parallel to the singing but not connected to it.

Below are three examples of how you could apply these methods. The song "Happy Birthday" is used as a song example.

1. Direct connection: While singing "Happy Birthday" out loud, play the rhythmic phrasing of the song using the floor tom, high tom, and snare drum. Invent variations on these three drums while sticking true to the rhythmic shape of the melody.

2. Abstract connection: Play fragments of the melody, stopping and starting while continuing to sing the song out loud. Add counter rhythms into the mix, reorchestrate your way around the drums, set up various timbres, and create ornamentations by adding outside elements that imply the melodic shape of the song, but not in a literal way.

3. Contrast: Play textures on the snare with brushes and play a Morse code pattern between left and right feet on the bass drum and high-hat while singing the melody out loud. Switch to mallets on the toms and play a figure that speeds up and slows down, adding occasional bass drum hits. Switch back to textural sounds on the snare with brushes. All of this happens out of time and is unrelated to the rhythmic content of your song.

12. SPACE

1.

Play any phrase on the drums.

Pause for at least twice as long as the length of your phrase.

Play a new phrase on the drums.

Pause for at least four times as long as your phrase length.

Play one more phrase on the drums.

Pause for at least eight times as long as the length of your phrase.

2.

Play a buzz roll on the snare drum.

Begin leaving small gaps of silence, then return to the roll.

The gaps of silence continue to grow in duration.

Soon, you will have as much silence as you will have sound.

Soon, the gaps of silence are more frequent and last longer than the sound.

End when you feel you should.

Form possibilities:

ABACA
ABABC
AABBAA
ABCABC
AB AB
ABCD
DCBA

13. ONE IDEA/ONE INSTRUMENT

Experiment with one idea for each instrument on the kit, and then improvise by adhering strictly to the ideas you have invented.

Some examples:

Right foot: bass drum
slow pulse/medium pulse/fast pulse/Morse code/isolated hits (loud or soft)

Right hand: snare drum/floor tom/rack tom/ride cymbal
texture/slow pulse/medium pulse/fast pulse/Morse code/one-handed roll/Morse code/cymbal overtones

Left foot: high-hat
steady pulse/uneven pulse/morse code/ isolated cymbal crashes

Left hand: snare drum/rack tom/crash cymbal
texture/slow pulse/medium pulse/fast pulse/Morse code/one-handed roll/Morse code/cymbal overtones

This is more of an exercise in "sound collage" than improvisation. But the benefits of focused concentration on four limbs working with four unrelated ideas can produce exciting results and inspire fresh perspectives that you can bring into a freely improvised context.

Additional options:

Develop two or more ideas for each instrument.

Begin with the right hand, add the left hand, add the left foot, and add the right foot.

Begin with the hands, then add the feet.

Begin with the feet, then add the hands.

What are some more ways you could apply this concept?

14. THE 20-BPM METRONOME EXERCISE REVISITED

Work through the metronome exercise from chapter 1 in this book with an added focus on dynamics.

1. Play as quietly as possible (*pp*).
2. Play as loud as possible (*ff*).
3. Gradual crescendo (*pp→ff*) during each repeat.
4. Gradual decrescendo (*ff→ff*) during each repeat.
5. Accent the first beat of each subdivision.
6. Accent the last beat of each subdivision.
7. Place random accents throughout the exercise.

15. RECORDINGS OF PERCUSSION MUSIC

I have listed several works available in a recorded format that feature percussion in some way, shape, or form. The stylistic range is vast, and the music was created in many different geographic locations. I have refrained from placing any of it into separate categories to avoid making unintentional divisions between, for example, "Western music" and "world music." It's all percussion music, and it's all fascinating. I have listed the recordings alphabetically.

Listen to and be inspired by this music, then use it to help develop new ideas on the drum set.

Note: We are not trying to steal anything here. We're listening to the material to help get the creative juices flowing. Absorb the sounds and assimilate them into your vocabulary in your own way.

There is an enormous amount of percussion-based music to explore, and the list I created is a drop in the bucket. One could spend a lifetime discovering new works. I encourage you to do your own independent research and check out as many sounds from as many places as you can.

Most of these recordings are in LP, CD, and digital formats. I recommend the Discogs website (www.discogs.com) as a great place to start looking. I have also included links to Bandcamp pages when applicable. Lastly, some of these works have multiple recordings made by various ensembles. In such cases, I list the title and the year of completion and leave it to you to search for and discover the many interpretations available.

Alhaji Ibrahim Abdulai, *Master Drummers of Dagbon, Vol 2* (Rounder CD 5046, 1990)
Balinese Gamelan, *Music of the Gamelan Gong Kebyar* (Vital Records, 1996)
Boubacar Diagne, *Tabala Wolof: Sufi Drumming of Senegal* (VPU 1002, 1992)
Cachao, *Cachao Y Su Descarga '77, Vol 1* (SAL 4111, 1977)
Capoeira, Samba, Candomble: Bahia / Brasil (Museum Collection Berlin, 1990)
Caroline Shaw, *Taxidermy* (https://sopercussion.bandcamp.com/track/taxidermy, 2012)
Edgar Varèse, *Ionisation* (1929-1931)
Folk Music of the Western Congo (Folkways Records FE 4427, 1961)
Gina Martin, *Santero–Cuban Cult Music Featuring Gina Martin, Vol. 2* (Panart, 1986)
Iannis Xenakis, *Persephassa* (1969)
Javanese Gamelan: Java Court Gamelan, Vol II (Nonesuch Explorer, 1977)
James Tenney, *Having Never Written a Note for Percussion* (1971)
Jennifer Higdon, *Splendid Wood* (2006)
American Music for Percussion 1 (Naxos–American Classics, 2011)
Johanna Beyer, *Percussion Suite* (1930)
John Cage, *First Construction in Metal* (1939)
Julia Perry, *Homunculus, C.F.* (1960)
Karlheinz Stockhausen, *No. 9: Zyklus, for solo percussion* (1959)
Lou Harrison, *Suite for Percussion* (1940)
Martinho Da Vila, *Martinho Da Vila* (1969)
Marvelous Boy: Calypso from West Africa (HJRLP 38, 2009)

Morton Feldman, *The King of Denmark* (1964)

Saikouba Badjie, *Bougarabou: Solo Drumming of Casamance* (VPU 1005, 1996)

Sissokho Yakhouba and Lansine Kouyate, *Mali: Kora & Balafon* (Air Mail Music SA 141126, 2006)

Sofia Gubaidulina, *In the Beginning There Was Rhythm* (1984)

Thundering Dragon: Percussion Music from China (Weltmusik, 1994)

William Winant, *Five American Percussion Pieces* (Poon Village, 2014)

Zakir Hussain, *Vikku Vinyakram–Super Percussion of India* (1991)

NOTES:

16. UNISONS

Invent a rhythmic pattern and repeat it for any length of time. This pattern can be in metered time or it can be a gesture that you repeat without an implied pulse. Use the method below and apply your invented pattern to it.

Play the pattern in unison with all four limbs on the drum set

(e.g., rh = ride cymbal, lh = snare drum, rf = bass drum, lf = high-hat).

Subtract one limb to make it a three-limb pattern.

Subtract one more to make it a two-limb pattern.

Subtract one more to make it a one-limb pattern.

And then:

Add one limb to make it a two-limb pattern.

Add one limb to make it a three-limb pattern.

Add one limb to make it a four-limb pattern.

Stick to one pattern while moving through a complete cycle of the exercise. Change rhythm only after the cycle is completed.

Additional options:

For those with a handle on reading traditional notation, I recommend the book Progressive Steps to Syncopation for the Modern Drummer *by Ted Reed. Use exercise 1 on page 38 and read the snare line as your rhythmic pattern. Repeat each line of the exercise while applying the method above.*

Move to exercises 2 through 8 (pp 39–45) and apply the unisons method.

What are some other ways you could apply the unison method to the syncopation exercises?

17. SOUND WALK

Here's a listening exercise to explore away from the drum set that I have found helpful in developing sensitive listening skills.

Go on a walk around your neighborhood, a nearby park, a riverfront, a hiking trail, a busy marketplace, a train station, or an airport. Stop at various moments during your walk and actively listen to the environment around you. Take as much time as you need.

Take a mental picture of the sounds heard. Write them in a notebook and/or record the sounds on your phone or a portable recording device during your walk. Keep them in a sound journal.

1.

Improvise on the drums using the sound walk as reference material. Be inspired by the sounds heard on your walk; don't try to imitate them necessarily; use the memory of the sounds to influence ideas on the drum set.

2.

If you recorded the sounds during your walk, listen to the field recordings with headphones and play along with the sounds. Make contrasting sounds, make similar sounds, leave space, and let the field recordings into the music.

In addition to helping develop sensitive and intentional listening, walking is also a great way to clear the mind and can help set a positive mental and physical environment in your practice room.

Is a daily routine of walking for at least 20 minutes a day before heading to the practice room in order?

18.BREATHING

1.

Take a deep breath. On an exhale, play freely around the drums until your breath runs out. Repeat the breathing exercise as much as you like. Explore the connection between breathing and sound. There should be an "ebb and flow" to the improvising using this concept, like waves hitting and receding on the shoreline.

2.

Breath in = improvise slow to fast phrases around the drum set. Breath out = improvise fast to slow phrases around the drum set.

3.

Improvise freely around the drums. Pause for one inhale and exhale. Pause for two inhales and two exhales. Pause for three inhales and three exhales (feel free to increase the number of breaths).

19. CROSSING FIELDS

Exploring content across multiple disciplines is a great way to inspire new ideas and concepts in your music. Interdisciplinary learning can have a tremendous impact by offering various viewpoints on a subject and, as a result, helping you think outside the box during the decision-making process.

There is an infinite body of work from many disciplines to choose from and be inspired by, and I encourage you to be curious and discover your own body of work from various fields of expression.

I have created a list below from the worlds of painting, sculpture, writing, photography, and filmmaking to provide a few examples of some of my cross-disciplinary heroes. What are some of the ways their work could influence sound-making?

PAINTERS AND SCULPTORS

Robert Rauschenberg
Eva Hesse
Jean-Michel Basquiat
Anthony Caro
Helen Frankenthaler
Laura Spong
Mike Williams
Agnes Martin
Theaster Gates
Sol Lewitt
Lee Krasner
Alexander Calder

WRITERS

James Joyce
George Orwell
Albert Camus
Harper Lee
James Baldwin
Pier Paolo Pasolini
Phillip Larkin
Anne Sexton
Robert Creeley
Susan Sontag
John Berger

Malcolm X
Hannah Arendt
Edward Said
Anton Chekov
Saul Bellow
John Irving

PHOTOGRAPHERS

Lee Friedlander
Vivian Maier
Gordon Parks
Saul Leiter
Sandy Steinbrecher
Ron Gordon
Helen Levitt
Diane Arbus

FILM MAKERS

John Cassavetes
Michael Snow
Chantal Akerman
Pier Paolo Pasolini
Stanley Kubrick
Claire Denis.

NOTES:

20. KNOW THYSELF

Let's figure out who you are.

This is the greatest challenge in life, and a lofty goal at that. The closer you come to knowing who you are as a human being, the better chance you will have of developing a unique voice on the drum set. There are no shortcuts. Stay curious, open to new ideas, and consistent with your practice routine.

"Be yourself; everyone else is taken" – Oscar Wilde

Hopefully, some of the ideas in this book will help get you there; the rest is up to you.

Enjoy the journey!

LISTENING GUIDE TO SOLO RECORDINGS

Below is a short list of solo drum set recordings that inspire me to continue my solo drum set practice. The music here is quite varied and offers a broad cross-section of what is possible on this instrument. The commonalities that tie these recordings together are the fact that the drum set was used in some way, shape, or form (even if augmented with small percussion, electronics, or other sound-making devices) and that the element of improvisation is inherent to the work to some degree. If the work is composed, the performer has a background in improvisation and has used this experience to influence the written work.

Even within these parameters, I'm sure I have left out many great recordings, with the repertoire for solo drum set music growing steadily. The ones I have listed here resonate highly with me, and I have listened to them repeatedly. Some of these recordings are easier to find than others. I recommend heading to the Discogs website (www.discogs.com) or buying directly from the artist's Bandcamp page (www.bandcamp.com) whenever possible.

Han Bennink, *Voor Masje* (ICP 011, 1974)
Han Bennink, *Solo–West/East* (FMP, 1979)
Scott Clark, *This Darkness* (OOYH 007, 2021)
Chris Corsano, *The Young Cricketer* (Family Vineyard, 2008)
Andrew Cyrille, *Music Delivery/Percussion* (Intakt Records, 2023)
Baby Dodds, *Talking and Drum Solos* (Folkways, 1951)
Hamid Drake, *Dedications* (Black Cross Solo Sessions: Corbett vs Dempsey, 2022)
Milford Graves, *Grand Unification* (Tzadik, 1998)
Devin Gray, *Most Definitely* (Rataplan Records, 2023)
Gerry Hemingway, *Solo Works* (Auricle Records/AUR–3, 1980)
Gerry Hemingway, *kernelings–solo works 1995–2012* (AUR 12 [CD], AUR 13 [DVD], 2014)
Susie Ibarra, *Drum Sketches* (Innova Recordings, 2007)
Susie Ibarra, *Rhythm Cycles / 7.11.19* (Otoroku, 2021)
Paul Lytton, *The Inclined Stick* (Po Torch Records, 1979)
Tatsuya Nakatani, *Primal Communication* (H&H Production HH-8, 2007)
Paal Nilssen – Love, *Miro* (PNL 007, 2010)
Frank Rosaly, *Milkwork* (Molk Records, 2010)
Chad Taylor, *Myths and Morals* (Eyes and Ears Records, 2018)
Vasco Trilla, *The Torch in My Ear* (Klopotec 2018)

CREATIVE SOLO MUSIC FOR THE DRUM SET · 41

LIVING HEROES

Below is an alphabetical list of drummers I have been lucky enough to have made contact with over the years and whose playing continues to inspire me to keep going with my music. The folks on this list come from a broad spectrum of genres and styles; however, all of them use improvisation to various degrees in their work. In addition, all the artists on this list are ones whom I have made a real-life connection with at some point: I may have heard them play live, shared a bill, had a conversation, taken a lesson, made a recording, driven in a car or train with them, interviewed them for the Option Series at Experimental Sound Studio here in Chicago, or all the above. Many incredible artists did not make the list, but this is only because I did not meet them in real life. Some of the artists on this list are also great composers and/or multi-instrumentalists, visual artists, writers, and deep thinkers in addition to being great drummers. I urge you to go and check out their work.

Barry Altschul	Devin Gray	Macio Moretti	Adam Shead
Mikel Patrick Avery	Luther Gray	Jon Mueller	Damon Short
Burkhard Beins	Ben Hall	Tim Mulvenna	Ted Sirota
Han Bennink	Dana Hall	Tatsuya Nakatani	Ståle Liavik Solberg
John Betsch	Bill Harris	John Niekrasz	Tyshawn Sorey
Dan Bitney	Steve Heather	Curt Newton	Erik Sowa
Jim Black	Gerry Hemingway	Kjell Nordeson	Isaiah Spencer
Katherina Bornefeld	John Herndon	Cyprian Pakuła	Kuba Suchar
Tony Buck	Steve Hunt	Randy Peterson	Phillip Sudderberg
Scott Clark	Sven-Åke Johansson	Kyle Gregory Price	Nori Tanaka
Gerald Cleaver	Didi Kern	Mike Pride	Chad Taylor
Chris Corsano	Quin Kirchner	Avreeayl Ra	Scott Dean Taylor
Jeremy Cunningham	Julian Kirshner	Tom Rainey	Vasco Trilla
Tyler Damon	Glenn Kotche	Mike Reed	Spencer Tweedy
Hamid Drake	Thymme Jones	Gino Robair	Michael Vatcher
Andrew Drury	Paal Nilssen –Love	Frank Rosaly	Nasheet Waits
Harris Eisenstadt	Paul Lovens	Claire Rousay	Matt Wilson
Marcus Evans	Paul Lytton	Charles Rumback	William Winant
Lily Finnegan	George Marich	Mark Sanders	Michael Zerang
Tomas Fujiwara	Makaya McCraven	Greg Saunier	Etienne Ziemniak
Jordan Glenn	Shannon Morrow	Ryan Sawyer	Liliana Zieniawa

RECOMMENDED READING

BOOKS

Derek Bailey, *Improvisation: It's Nature and Practice in Music* (Da Capo Press, 1992)

Matt Brennan, *Kick It: A Social History of the Drumset* (Oxford University Press, 2022)

Stephanie Stein Crease, *Rhythm Man: Chick Webb and the Beat That Changed America* (Oxford University Press, 2023)

Larry Gara, *The Baby Dodds Story: As Told to Larry Gara* (Rebeats, 2003)

Terrie Hessels and Emma Fischer, *Improvising: A One-Year Journey around Africa* (Terp Records, 2021)

George E. Lewis, *A Power Stronger Than Itself: The AACM and American Experimental Music* (University of Chicago Press, 2008)

Graham Lock, *Forces in Motion: The Music and Thoughts of Anthony Braxton* (Da Capo Press, 1988)

Joe Morris, *Perpetual Frontier: The Properties of Free Music* (Riti, 2012)

Bob Ostertag, *Creative Life: Music Politics People and Machines* (University of Illinois Press, 2009)

Edwin Prévost, *An Uncommon Music for The Common Man: A Polemical Memoir* (Copula, 2020)

Steven Schick, *The Percussionist's Art: Same Bed, Different Dreams* (University of Rochester Press, 2006)

Salomé Voegelin, *Listening to Noise and Silence: Towards a Philosophy of Sound Art* (Continuum, 2011)

ARTICLES AND INTERVIEWS

"The Birth of the Drum Set," *Smithsonian Music,* June 2015
https://music.si.edu/story/birth-drum-set

"Free Jazz Does Not Exist: An Interview with Han Bennink of Instant Composers Pool," *The Thin Air*, Brian Coney, November 2017
https://thethinair.net/2017/11/han-bennink/

"Milford Graves: Sounding the Universe," *New Music USA/New Music Box,* Aakash Mittal, February 1, 2018
https://newmusicusa.org/nmbx/milford-graves-sounding-the-universe/

"Seven Interviews with Andrew Cyrille," *The Public Archive: black history in white times*, December 6, 2015
https://thepublicarchive.com/?p=4677

"Documenting Percussionist Susie Ibarra's Mesmerizing Rhythms," *In Sheep's Clothing Hi-Fi*, E. Little, March 16, 2022
https://insheepsclothinghifi.com/susie-ibarra/

Mexico City :: 2018
Photo by Tim Daisy

(photo by Steve Kaiser)

Tim Daisy is a Chicago-based drummer, composer, and presenter who has been active in the improvised music scene since the late 1990s. He owns and operates Relay Recordings, which documents
his solo and collaborative work with artists and ensembles from around North America and Europe.
He lives in Evanston, IL, with his partner Emma, children Lewis and Nina, and a cat named Rizzo.

WWW.TIMDAISY.WORDPRESS.COM

WWW.TIMDAISYRELAYRECORDS.BANDCAMP.COM

CONTACT: TIMDAISY@HOTMAIL.COM